Ko-hoh: The Call of the
Trumpeter Swan

Ko-hoh: The Call of the Trumpeter Swan

by Jay Featherly

A Carolrhoda Nature Watch Book

Carolrhoda Books, Inc./Minneapolis

Maps based on material from
A Management Plan for Trumpeter Swans in Alberta, 1982
by Steven Brechtel, for Alberta Energy and
Natural Resources, Fish and Wildlife Division

LIBRARY OF CONGRESS CATALOGING-IN-PUBLICATION DATA

Featherly, Jay.
   Ko-hoh: the call of the trumpeter swan.

   "A Carolrhoda nature watch book."
   Summary: Explains the life cycle of the world's
largest swan, including information on nest-building,
mating, the raising of young, feeding, and other
behavior.
   1. Trumpeter swan—Juvenile literature.
[1. Trumpeter swan. 2. Swans] I. Title.
QL696.A52F38   1986   598.4'1   85-30955
ISBN 0-87614-288-9 (lib. bdg.)

1 2 3 4 5 6 7 8 9 10 96 95 94 93 92 91 90 89 88 87 86

Swans are the largest and most majestic of all waterfowl. With their snow-white feathers and long, curved necks, these beautiful birds are easy to recognize on water, land, and in the air. It is thrilling to see a swan pair gliding gracefully across a calm pond or quiet lake, or a flock of swans flying on powerful wings against the blue sky.

Different kinds of swans live on every continent of the world except Africa. Two **species**, or kinds, of swans are native to North America. The tundra swan, which also lives in Europe and Asia, is the most common. This book is about the much rarer trumpeter swan, the one swan species that lives only in North America.

The trumpeter swan is the world's largest swan. With its neck extended, the male bird measures 5 feet (1.5 m) from bill to tail, and it sometimes weighs over 30 pounds (13.6 kg). Its wings can span 8 feet (2.4 m) from tip to tip. Female trumpeters are a few inches shorter and average five pounds lighter than the males. The **plumage**, or feathering, of adult birds is pure white, but the feathers on the head and neck of trumpeter swans are usually stained a rusty color. This stain comes from minerals and decaying plants

found in the water and marsh mud where swans dip their heads to feed.

The trumpeter swan was named for its voice—and no wonder! Its call is the loudest of any bird in North America. Its deep-toned "ko-hoh" sounds much like a horn. In fact, for the Kootenai Indian tribe of western Canada, *ko-hoh* was the word for swan. Trumpeter swans call often, both while flying and when on the water. A swan produces the loud call by forcing air from its lungs through its very long windpipe.

There are four major trumpeter swan **nesting grounds**, or areas where swans build their nests and breed. Most spend the summer in southern Alaska, where they are rarely seen. Other important summer homes for the trumpeters exist in the province of Alberta in western Canada and in the lower Yukon Territory between Alaska and British Columbia. The best place to watch and study trumpeter swans, however, is in

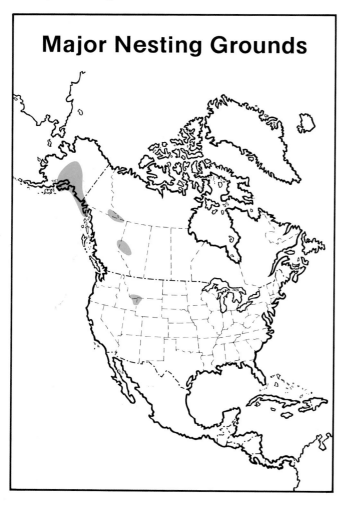

Major Nesting Grounds

the Rocky Mountain region surrounding Yellowstone National Park. This nesting ground covers portions of Wyoming, Montana, and Idaho. The photographs in this book were taken in and around this area.

The trumpeter swan was once much more common than it is today. For many thousands of years it nested over most of northern North America. Indians

for making powder puffs, quilts, and pillows. The **quills**, or long, stiff feathers, were made into writing pens.

By the early 1900s, many experts believed the great swans would soon become **extinct**, or disappear completely. Although laws protecting the swans were introduced, **poachers**, or people hunting illegally, continued to capture and shoot the birds.

killed a small number of swans. They used swan meat for food, the swan feathers to decorate special clothes, and the bones to make beads.

The Indians did not affect the swan population significantly, but then, during the 1800s, the swan population began to drop. White hunters and trappers killed thousands of swans. Many white people wanted the swan feathers

Despite their decreasing numbers, a few small flocks still struggled to survive in hidden marshes. In 1932, only 69 trumpeter swans were counted in the United States. Most were found in Yellowstone Park and at the Red Rock Lakes in southern Montana. The Yellowstone birds were well protected, but the swans outside the park were still being shot illegally during duck-hunting season. In 1935, the federal government decided to do something to stop the illegal swan hunting. The 40,000-acre (16,000-hectare) Red Rock Lakes National Wildlife Refuge was established, where people would be kept at least a quarter of a mile from nesting swans at all times. This way, people could watch the swans without disturbing them. Hunting, of course, was absolutely forbidden. These rules are still in effect today.

Undisturbed by humans, the swans made a rapid comeback on the vast marshes and shallow lakes inside the refuge. In just 20 years, the small flock grew to nearly 400 birds. Hundreds more lived outside the refuge. Other trumpeter flocks protected in Canada were also increasing, and scientists discovered several previously unknown nesting grounds in Alaska.

Humans have also helped the swan population by returning trumpeters to some of their former nesting areas to start new flocks. Eggs and young swans have been **transplanted**, or moved, from Red Rock Lakes to Carver Park Reserve in Minnesota and LaCreek National Wildlife Refuge in South Dakota. Now these transplanted swans are spreading into nearby states. A few trumpeters have also been transplanted into Oregon and Nevada.

Now that trumpeter swans are successfully breeding in these new locations, people and nature together have saved the trumpeter swan from extinction. Almost 10,000 of these magnificent birds are alive today, nesting and raising their young.

Young adult trumpeters usually choose a mate during their third winter. The male and female form a strong **pair bond**, and they will stay together until one of the swans dies. Following their instincts, the pair may begin building a nest in the spring, but they often abandon it and don't raise a family for one to three more years.

A trumpeter pair begins defending its **territory**, or area it will protect as its own, in early spring. Swans need a large nesting territory. Each pair claims an entire small lake or portion of marsh in which to raise its young. A nesting area can be as small as a 9-acre (3.6-hectare) lake, or as large as 70 to 150 acres (28 to 60 hectares) of marshland. There must be plenty of shallow water filled with marsh plants to feed a growing swan family through the summer.

Both birds chase away any other swans that trespass on their territory. Because trumpeters mate for life, a single pair of swans may claim the same lake or portion of marsh each year.

Once the last snow has melted, the birds begin nesting. Trumpeter swans build their large, bulky nests on top of abandoned muskrat houses or in thick beds of marsh plants. Sometimes they use a small island or beaver lodge as a nest site. The swans choose a place where the surrounding water or deep mud will make it difficult for other animals to approach and eat their eggs.

The male and female work together to form the nest mound. The male swan, called a **cob**, pulls plants from the bottom of the marsh with his bill. He then stretches his long neck and passes them toward his mate. The female, or **pen**, stands on the mound and arranges the plants with her bill until the nest is about 18 inches (46 cm) above the water. The finished nest mound measures 6 or 7 feet (about 2 m) across at the bottom. The pen then scoops out a hollow for her eggs with her broad webbed feet. It takes the birds up to two weeks to build a new nest, but older trumpeter pairs often just spend a few days repairing the last year's nest before egg laying begins.

The swans mate several times while the nest is being built. Swans mate in the water. To mate, the male trumpeter climbs onto the female's back and deposits his **sperm**, or male reproductive cells, into her body. She is then able to lay **fertilized eggs** in which young swans will develop.

The pen lays her eggs in early May. An average **clutch**, or group of eggs in a nest, is four or five eggs, but some females lay up to nine. One egg is laid every other day. Once she has laid all her eggs, she begins sitting on the nest.

In the weeks before egg laying, the pen eats a great deal of food to build up extra fat in her body. This fat will help nourish her during the **incubation period**, the time during which the eggs must be kept warm so that they will hatch. A swan incubates her eggs for 33 to 37 days. Even with her extra fat, she must still leave the eggs daily to find food. When she does, the cob often remains nearby to guard the nest.

While his mate is incubating, the cob continues to defend their territory fiercely. His instinct to protect the nest is so strong that he will attack even harmless animals that wander near it. Male trumpeters have even been known

20

to rush at large animals, such as elk and moose, that are feeding near the nest.

A swan must be more cautious when a dangerous **predator**, or animal that can catch and eat swans, enters its territory. If a threatening animal such as a bear or a coyote enters the territory, a swan will swim a safe distance away, trumpeting single notes of alarm. Only when a hungry predator actually threatens the swans' eggs will the cob risk trying to frighten it away.

Most trumpeter swans will not defend their nest against humans. So as with dangerous animal predators, the pair simply swims away until the people are gone. Certain swans in Yellowstone Park are so used to seeing people that they lose some of this great fear of human beings. Then, when someone approaches too near the incubating female, one or both swans may rush forward and strike at the person with the hard front edges of the wings.

It is important to watch nesting trumpeter swans from a distance. If the birds are disturbed too often, they will become frightened and abandon their eggs.

When other trumpeter swans invade the territory, the pen often joins her mate in defending it. Together, the pair swims toward the trespassers, calling a loud warning. If the other swans ignore the warning, the pair flaps across the water in a furious attack. If the angry pair catches the trespassers, they bite

the intruders' wings and pull their tail feathers. Once the trespassing swans escape into the air, the cob may chase them far beyond the pair's territory.

When the male trumpeter returns and lands triumphantly near the nest, his mate joins him. Now that they have successfully defended their territory, the cob and pen face each other and perform a **triumph display**. For a few moments they trumpet excitedly and quiver their outstretched wings.

Because trumpeter swans guard their clutches so carefully, few eggs are lost to predators. There are some dangers, however, that the birds cannot control. Every year, many eggs are destroyed by floods in the nesting grounds. Also, for reasons not entirely understood, some pens lay **infertile** eggs. These are eggs in which an **embryo**, or developing swan, is not present. Sometimes an embryo does develop, but the baby swan is too weak to break through its thick shell at hatching time. Usually, however, two out of every three eggs do hatch.

Most baby swans hatch in late June. Their parents hear the unborn young peeping inside their shells. It takes 1½ to 2 days for all the eggs to hatch. During this time, the mother swan stays on the nest constantly.

The swan baby uses an **egg tooth**, a hard, pointed knob on the tip of its bill, to break free of the egg. With the strong muscles in its tiny neck, the unborn bird presses the egg tooth outward until small holes are broken through the thick eggshell. At last a complete ring is broken around the egg. The shell separates, and in moments the young swan, called a **cygnet** (SIG-net), wriggles free.

Cygnets hatch from the egg with their eyes wide open and their bodies covered with damp, downy feathers. Newly hatched trumpeter swans weigh almost 8 ounces (227 g). Their pale-gray down quickly dries and fluffs out. Within one hour they are able to sit upright and begin moving around the nest hollow. The pen will often lift her body several inches above the nest to look at her young underneath. The cygnets stare back.

This first contact between a cygnet and one of its parents is vital to the young bird's survival. The cygnet doesn't know it is a trumpeter swan when it hatches. When it first looks at the female swan, the cygnet recognizes her as its parent and will then know later to follow her and the male trumpeter when the family leaves the nest. The process of young birds and other animals learning to identify their parents is called **imprinting**.

Parent trumpeters do not bring food to their young on the nest. Cygnets can survive for their first several days without feeding. This is because their bodies still carry some of the **yolk**, the nutritious substance inside the egg, that nourished them before they hatched.

Before the newly hatched cygnets are strong enough to leave the nest, the parent trumpeters fiercely protect their young. Both the pen and cob stand firmly on the nest mound when an enemy approaches. The swans spread their wings to make themselves appear huge and threatening. They hiss loudly to add to their threatening display. Few enemies will risk challenging an angry trumpeter swan pair that is defending a young brood.

A trumpeter family usually begins making short feeding trips into the marsh on the cygnets' second or third day. The young birds quickly become greedy feeders. During the first few weeks of their lives, the cygnets feed mostly on insects, water beetles, snails, and freshwater shrimp. These tiny water creatures are stirred up to the surface by the parent swans, who feed on water plants pulled up from the marsh bottom.

The cygnets dart around their parents and snap up the food. Soon they add bits of stirred-up water plants to their diet, too. Then at three or four weeks of age, when their necks have grown several inches, the young birds begin pulling up water plants on their own. Swans feed by "tipping up"—going head-first under the water, leaving their tail ends sticking up—the way ducks do.

The trumpeter family keeps close together as they travel about their territory in the marsh. The pen and cob keep a sharp watch for the many predators—otters and mink, gulls, eagles, ravens, or coyotes—that will quickly prey on an unprotected young bird. The family visits feeding places where the water is shallow enough for the cygnets to reach food. At first they rest for the night on the nest. Then after a month or so, the new family ranges further into its territory and sleeps at favorite places on the shore. They choose sleeping spots where predators cannot easily approach without being spotted by the alert adult swans.

At six weeks the cygnets' first feathers appear, replacing the soft down that has covered their bodies since hatching. By ten weeks they have all their feathers, except for the last of their flight feathers. Their plumage at this stage is a handsome dark gray with whitish underparts. Their wing feathers are white, and their bills are beginning to turn black. At just ten weeks of age, trumpeter swan cygnets weigh almost 15 pounds (6.8 kg).

During the summer, adult trumpeter swans **molt**, or shed, their wing feathers. Swans lose all their flight feathers at once, so they are unable to fly for about one month before their new wing feathers grow in. While flight- less, trumpeters without young gather in flocks on large lakes where they are safe from predators. Molting swans can only flap their ragged wings and struggle across the water to escape from danger.

Trumpeter pairs with cygnets molt differently. The pen usually sheds her flight feathers soon after the cygnets hatch, while the cob molts his later in the summer. By molting at different times, one of the parent swans is always able to fly and defend the family while the young birds are growing up.

Like all birds, swans take good care of their feathers. Immediately after bathing, the birds carefully **preen**, or clean and smooth, their feathers. Using its bill, the swan collects oil from the **preen gland** at the base of its tail and rubs the oil on its feathers. The oil waterproofs the swan's feathers and helps to keep them in good condition.

The nearly grown cygnets begin to exercise and develop their flight muscles. They flap their wings while bathing and when chasing each other across the water in play. This is important exercise because soon the young trumpeters must learn to fly.

Ice and snow will soon cover the nesting grounds for the long winter. So by autumn, the cygnets must be ready to **migrate**, or fly to warmer places for the winter. When their cygnets are about 100 days old, the cob and pen suddenly begin bobbing their heads and trumpeting. With this signal, the young birds begin swimming around in excitement. For several days they have practiced flapping across the water, beating

their newly feathered wings with all their strength. Now they are finally able to fly. When the adult birds take off over the water, the cygnets are able to follow.

Each day the trumpeter family makes several of these practice flights to prepare the cygnets for the migration southward. Within a week, the young birds are circling above the nesting grounds on strong wings, now able to fly for miles.

When early snows begin falling, the trumpeter swans leave their summer territories and travel in small flocks toward the wintering grounds. They fly in irregular V formations and slanted lines across the sky. The Alaskan trumpeters winter along 1,000 miles (1,609 km) of the Pacific coast as far south as Washington state. Swans from the Canadian nesting grounds travel to a much smaller wintering area. They arrive in the Yellowstone National Park region in late October and spend the winter on ponds and rivers fed by **hot springs.** Here, high in the Rocky Mountains, blizzards rage and winter temperatures may drop to -50 degrees F (-45 degrees C), but the swans remain comfortable on the warm waters despite the severe weather.

With good winter **habitat**, or areas in which to live, available nearby, the trumpeter swans of Yellowstone and Red Rock Lakes do not migrate at all. They gather in flocks with the Canadian birds wherever there is open water rich in choice food. In the winter, the swans have no reason to defend territories, so they live together peacefully.

The cygnets continue to grow and change during the winter. Their voices develop from weak toots to hoarse imitations of the adult birds. Their feathers begin to turn white. By next summer, they will have the pure white plumage and full voice of mature trumpeter swans.

The cold months pass. Spring is near. The young birds must leave their parents and fend for themselves. Two winters later, they will pair with mates and in another year or two begin nesting. If they escape the dangers of disease, predators, and accidents, these young trumpeters will live over 20 years and raise perhaps a dozen cygnet broods in their lifetime. As their numbers continue to increase, the trumpetlike "ko-hoh" of this beautiful white swan will echo across North America for years to come.

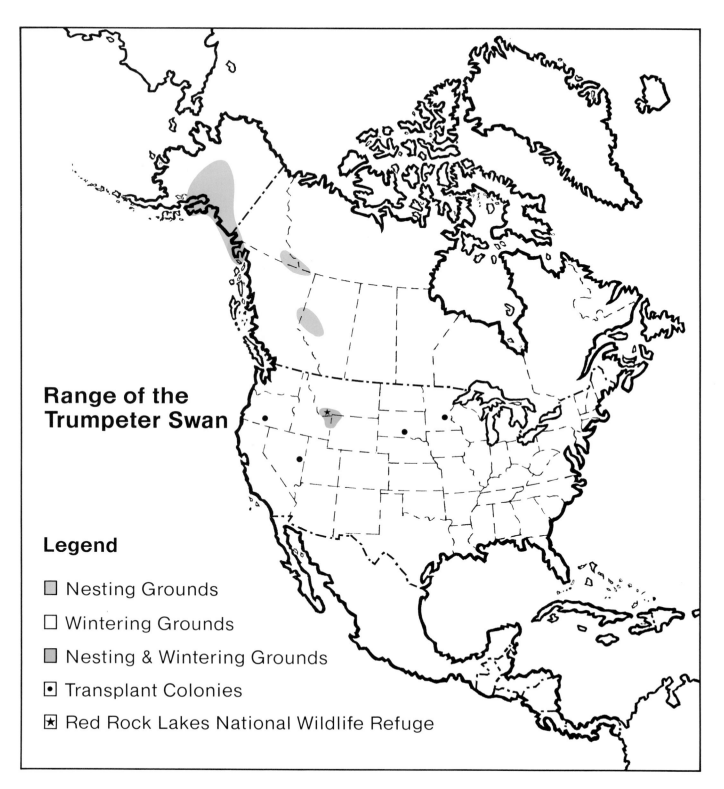

Range of the Trumpeter Swan

Legend

- ☐ Nesting Grounds
- ☐ Wintering Grounds
- ☐ Nesting & Wintering Grounds
- ⊡ Transplant Colonies
- ⊠ Red Rock Lakes National Wildlife Refuge

GLOSSARY

clutch: the group of eggs in a nest

cob: a male swan

cygnet: a swan less than one year old

egg tooth: a hard, pointed knob on the tip of a bird's bill, used for breaking out of the shell at hatching time

embryo: a developing bird or animal before birth

extinct: When all the animals of one kind, or species, die, that animal is extinct.

fertilized egg: an egg that contains an embryo

habitat: a place where an animal or plant naturally lives or grows

hot spring: a spring with water above 98 degrees F (37 degrees C)

imprinting: the process of a newborn bird or other animal learning to identify its parent

incubation period: the period of time it takes for eggs to become ready to hatch

infertile: when an egg does not contain an embryo

migrate: to move to a new living area, usually seasonally, for feeding or breeding

molt: to shed old feathers and grow new ones

nesting grounds: the area where birds build their nests and breed

pair bond: when male and female animals stay together to breed and raise young

pen: a female swan

plumage: the feathers covering a bird's body

poacher: a person who hunts illegally

predator: an animal that kills other animals for food

preen: to clean and smooth the feathers

preen gland: a gland that secretes an oil that waterproofs a bird's feathers

quills: long, stiff feathers, usually on the wings and tail

species: a group of plants or animals that share similar characteristics

sperm: male reproductive cells

territory: the area of land or water claimed and protected by an animal as its own

transplant: to move from one place and settle elsewhere

triumph display: the behavior of a swan pair after defending the nesting territory

yolk: the nutritious substance inside an egg that feeds a developing embryo

ABOUT THE AUTHOR

Jay Featherly grew up in Wyoming and has had a keen interest in wildlife since childhood. He began taking pictures of animals with a box camera when he was ten years old. Currently he photographs and writes about nature professionally. Swans and wild horses have been his most recent animal subjects. *Ko-hoh: The Call of the Trumpeter Swan* is his first Carolrhoda Nature Watch Book.